BOHDAN IHOR ANTONYCH

THE GRAND HARMONY

Translated by Michael M. Naydan

Glagoslav Publications

THE GRAND HARMONY

by Bohdan Ihor Antonych

Translated by **Michael M. Naydan**

Publishers Maxim Hodak & Max Mendor

© 2017, Michael M. Naydan

© 2017, Glagoslav Publications, United Kingdom

Glagoslav Publications Ltd
88-90 Hatton Garden
EC1N 8PN London
United Kingdom

www.glagoslav.com

ISBN: 978-1-911414-35-3

This book is in copyright. No part of this publication may be reproduced, stored in a retrieval system or transmitted in any form or by any means without the prior permission in writing of the publisher, nor be otherwise circulated in any form of binding or cover other than that in which it is published without a similar condition, including this condition, being imposed on the subsequent purchaser.

BOHDAN IHOR ANTONYCH

THE GRAND HARMONY

Translated by Michael M. Naydan

*This edition is dedicated to
Lydia Stefanowska, an expert
on Antonych par excellence.*

Bohdan Ihor Antonych

(1909-1937)

Biographical Note

The remarkable Ukrainian poet and literary critic Bohdan Ihor Antonych (1909-1937) lived for only a brief 28 years. Originally from the mountainous Lemko region in Poland, where a variant of Ukrainian is spoken, he was home-schooled for the first eleven years of his life until 1920 when he entered the Queen Sophia State Gymnasium in Syanok, which he completed eight years later. Antonych then matriculated at Lviv University. Lviv is the cultural center of Western Ukraine, which in Antonych's lifetime was part of Poland. During his study of Ukrainian philology at the university, Antonych adopted Ukrainian as his literary language, and he also became extremely active in the literary and intellectual life of the multi-cultural city of Lviv, a city that he grew to love dearly. Antonych served as a kind of cultural bridge between Polish and Ukrainian literary circles, which at the time did not mix to any great degree. He died in 1937 of complications from pneumonia after a successful operation for appendicitis, just a few short months before his planned wedding to Olha Oliynyk. His premature death occurred at the height of his creative talent, when he already had emerged as a poet of extraordinary maturity and erudition.

In the brief span of his life, Antonych proved to have been an exceptionally innovative poet and an accomplished essayist. As Lydia Stefanowska observes in her critical writings on the poet, Antonych was greatly influenced by Polish avant-garde poetry of the 1920s and was one of the first literary critics to note the talent of the then young future Nobel Prize winner Czeslaw Milosz. Antonych's poetry was a breath of fresh air for Ukrainian poetry in the 1930s, and like a number great poets, he was perceived in many different ways by his reading public. He has been described as an imagist, a mystic, a symbolist, and a pantheist. While these labels may fit certain moments in his poetry, they do not individually convey the totality of his oeuvre. His relatively small corpus of published works has been extraordinarily influential on a number of Ukrainian poets for generations to come, especially during the periods of the 1960s and 1980s, which were particularly trying times for Ukrainian society under Soviet repression. Antonych's poetry covers a number of themes from the mundane, the joy of life in little things, to the profoundly metaphysical, to nature and man's place in it, to urban themes, to an impending sense of apocalypse, which, regrettably, came true with the Nazi invasion. As opposed to the patriotic tendencies of a number of Western Ukrainian poets in his time, Antonych's approach was an art for art's sake one with high-minded aesthetic principles. His published collections include: *A Greeting to Life* (1931), *Three Rings* (1934), *The Book of the Lion* (1936), *The Green Gospel* (1938), and *Rotations* (1938). The latter two books were published posthumously. *The Grand Harmony*, a collection of poems on religious themes written in 1932, is a subtle and supple examination of the journey to personal faith, with all its revelatory verities and questioning. During Soviet times it was banned for its religious content. It was first published in its entirety in 1967 in New York.

The Grand Harmony first appeared in my English translation in a bilingual edition with Litopys Publishers in 2007, which has long been sold out. The poems "Musica Noctis," "De Morte I," "Ars Poetica 1" and "Liber Peregrinorum 3" were reprinted in my translation in *The Essential Poetry of Bohdan Ihor Antonych: Ecstasies and Elegies* (Bucknell University Press, 2010). One can find additional poetic renderings of Antonych's selected poetry in the translations of various well-known American poets under the title *A Square of Angels* (Ann Arbor: Ardis Publishers, 1977), which was edited by Bohdan Boychuk.

    I am grateful to Mykhailo Komarnytsky and Myroslava Prykhoda for all their support and assistance to make that original volume possible. I am especially thankful to Lydia Stefanowska for sharing her expertise on Antonych with me and for helping to make these translations better. My gratitude also to Mykola Polyuha for his expert suggestions for emendations. My translations for this new edition have been revised and fine-tuned from the original published versions.

Antonych Writing God: The Metaphysics of The Grand Harmony

The term metaphysical poetry has no clear-cut substantive definition in the criticism, but rather approximations and sometimes ad hoc generalizations. Its ineluctability should come as no surprise, since by its very nature it ought to be intuited and unquantifiable. Metaphysical poetry often attempts to be mimetic of the mystical experience. The reader intuits the metaphysical by co-experiencing the process of mystical transport with the poet. The central paradox lies in the question of how one can manage to describe the unknowable and the unseen within the limitations of human language in a three-dimensional world. Try as they did, the Symbolists, many of them beginning with or lapsing into decadence, never resolved this issue. As astute an observer and practitioner of the metaphysical arts as T.S. Eliot has admitted the monumental difficulty and perhaps impossibility of the task. Donning the hat of critic in discussing the disparate works of the 17th century English Metaphysical Poets (Donne, Marvell, Cleveland, Cowley, Crashaw, Herbert, and Vaughn), Eliot once declared that "not only is it difficult to define metaphysical poetry, but difficult to decide what poets practise it and in which of their verses."[1] He further remarks that "it is difficult to find any precise use of metaphor, simile, or other conceit, which is common to all the poets and at the same time important enough as an element of style to isolate these poets as a group."[2]

Bohdan Ihor Antonych's second collection of poetry *The Grand Harmony* (1932-1933), which the poet did not publish in his prematurely shortened lifespan, openly qualifies as a sustained metaphysical quest by the twenty-two year old poet to come to a deeper understanding of the nature of God as well as his personal and poetic relationship to Him. The collection fits into the rich tradition of Ukrainian religious poetry and, in fact, echoes certain elements of Hryhory Skovoroda's *Garden of Divine Songs* as well as imagery from some of the early religious-toned poetry of Pavlo Tychyna. The poems of *The Grand Harmony*, however, do not share the highly structured order of other religious mystical poetry such as that of St. Theresa of Avila and St. John of the Cross, whose poetry has a typical meditative sequence consisting of 1) meditative quiet; 2) darkness and terror; 3) mystic transport; and 4) revelation. Antonych's poems in his collection are more personal and intellectual and largely about the poet's traversal between faith and doubt within the symbolic system of organized religion (the church and the Divine Liturgy), the Bible, other religious writings, and most importantly for Antonych—the art of poetry

---

1   T.S. Eliot, "The Metaphysical Poets," in *The Metaphysical Poets*, Frank Kermode, ed. (Greenwich, CT: Fawcett, 1966), 126.

2   Eliot, 127.

and the perception of inspiration as divine. The collection, in fact, to a great degree, is an attempt at synthesis of personal religious belief with the metaphysics of poetry and poetic inspiration.

Before examining the collection in greater detail, I should make certain observations regarding a few problematic issues. First, the collection was never published in Antonych's lifetime and existed only in manuscript form before Antonych's close friend poet and icon painter Sviatoslav Hordynsky and poet-scholar Bohdan Rubchak first published it in 1967.[3] Therefore its incompleteness in Antonych's mind and tentative structure can only be taken as only partially indicative of Antonych's aesthetic design—although the order of its components may very well have been very close to his final poetic intent. Seven of the poems were published individually in separate issues of the Ukrainian Greek Catholic journal *Dzvony*—six in 1932 and one in 1933. Scholars have speculated on why Antonych chose not to publish the collection, suggesting its incompleteness as the primary reason and possibly the fact that he considered his collections *Try persteni* (Three Rings; 1934) and *Knyha leva* (Book of the Lion; 1936) as well as his posthumously published collections *Zelena Ievanheliia* (The Green Gospel; 1938) and *Rotatsii* (Rotations; 1938) poetically much more advanced. While this certainly may be true, *The Grand Harmony* does represent a remarkable maturation and development in Antonych's poetics from his first collection of juvenilia *Pryvitannia zhyttia* (A

---

3   Bohdan Ihor Antonych. *Zibrani tvory*. Ed. Sviatoslav Hordynsky and Bohdan Rubchak. New York and Winnepeg: Slovo, 1967.

Greeting to Life; 1931). Antonych's self-perception of the collection's transitional nature within his poetics thus may have additionally contributed to him not publishing it. I might add that his later poetry also engaged a more subtle poetics and took a turn from the kind of intense saturation of traditional religious imagery found in *The Grand Harmony*. The simplest explanation, however, might be that Antonych's constant ill health along with the turbulent times of the mid-to-late 1930s may have kept him from publishing it—as happened with two other of his collections.

At this point I will turn my attention to certain structural aspects of the collection. Its title *The Grand Harmony* echoes elements of ancient philosophy as well as the Enlightenment religious tradition. The modifier "velykyi" (great or grand) is a standard way to describe God as well as personages of high status such as princes and kings. The notion of harmony in the title suggests the Pythagorean idea of the harmony or the music of the spheres, which Aristotle describes as follows: "… all things seemed to be modeled on numbers, and numbers seemed to be the first things in the whole of nature, they supposed the elements of number to be the elements of all things, and the whole heaven to be a musical scale and a number."[4] Plato was later to use this idea in his *Republic* when he wrote the following about the cosmos: "…Upon each of its circles stood a siren who was carried round with its

---

4   http://www.dartmouth.edu/~matc/math5.geometry/unit3/unit3.html

movements, uttering the concords of a single scale...."[5] And Johannes Kepler in his *Harmonice Mundi* (1619), in linking mathematics and astronomy with God, observed that he intends "to erect the magnificent edifice of the harmonic system of the musical scale ... as God, the Creator Himself, has expressed it in harmonizing the heavenly motions."[6] Thus the notion of the harmony of the cosmos and the link of that notion with God certainly long preceded Antonych's title. The idea additionally has a lengthy lineage in its literary manifestations from Dante and later Milton to the present day. One should also point out the fact that Antonych received considerable musical training on the violin, and, one would surmise, in choral music as the son of a rural priest in Lemkivshchyna and at the gymnasium he attended in Syanok, which he completed in 1928.[7] Thus, given the poet's strong classical background in Greek and Latin, which he began to study while being home-schooled during a childhood beset by illness, and his passion for music, the concept of harmony acquires a particular point of intensity for the poet.

---

[5]   http://www.dartmouth.edu/~matc/math5.geometry/unit3/unit3.html

[6]   http://www.dartmouth.edu/~matc/math5.geometry/unit3/unit3.html

[7]   In his introduction to the *Zibrani tvory* edition, Sviatoslav Hordynsky observes that Antonych played well enough to perform solo on the violin at a Shevchenko concert and penned several musical compositions, including a march sung by his entire gymnasium cohort (9).

The poems in the collection are dated largely between March 23-June 3, 1932 with a few penned between March 24-26, 1933. The dates mostly correspond to the Lenten Fast and Easter season. Easter according to the Gregorian calendar was May 1 in 1932 and April 16 in 1933. According to the Julian calendar it was April 18 in 1932 and on April 3 in 1933. Thus the approaching Easter holiday, with its focus on Christ's death and resurrection as well as the source for human salvation, provided the stimulus during those two years for Antonych to write his meditations on God. When one examines the titles of the 45 poems in the collection, 38 of them appear in Latin or Greek and 7 in Ukrainian. A number of the Latin titles come from elements of the Roman Catholic Latin mass, a tradition in which Antonych grew up in the Lemko region as the son of a rural Catholic priest Vasyl Kit, who changed the family name to Antonych. "Kit" means "cat" in Ukrainian.

The sequence in the Latin mass of its five invariable hymns consists of: 1) Kyrie Eleison, 2) Gloria in Excelsis, 3) Credo, 4) Sanctus, and 5) Agnus Dei. All five of these hymns comprise titles in the collection, though in a different order than found in the mass. Most strikingly the Greek Gregorian chant Kyrie Eleison (Lord Have Mercy) is located toward the end of the collection, followed by three poems—"Magnificat," "Ars poetica" and "Salve Regina." *The Grand Harmony*, in fact, is saturated with imagery from the Latin mass including prayers, psalms, and songs, especially Gregorian chant, the latter of which was prevalent in the Tridentine liturgy until the reforms of Vatican II. Note titles such as "Veni Sancta Spiritus," "Amen," "Deus Magnificus," "Te Deum Laudamus," "Veni Creator," "Confiteor," "Mater Dolorosa," "Credo," "Mater Gloriosa," and "Salve Regina." Thus a considerable part of the collection is centered on liturgical musical forms that provide a point of focus for Antonych's meditations.

Musical metaphors also abound in the collection. For the sake of brevity I will give just a few examples. In the poem "Musica Noctis," Antonych's persona writes: "The distance echoes with just barely audible harps,/wind tunes the night by the tuning fork of God (lines 7-8)." At the end of the poem he likens God to a great pianist: "Let us listen to the great concert in the evening as/God places his hands on the piano of the world" (15-16). In "Deus Magnificus," whose title comes from Psalm 18 of the Latin Bible ("quantum Deus sit magnificus" – "the firmament shows us how magnificent God is"), Antonych ends with the following quatrain:

> He gives melody to every thing.
> He is harmony, He is a musical chord,
> He is the tuning fork tuning your heart,
> He is Perfect, Majestic Sound. (13-16)

The poet throughout the collection is an instrument played by God—whether a violin, harps, lyres, pipes, or a voice inspired to sing God's praises. In the poem "Magnificat" Antonych writes:

> O heart, sing a psalm of praise to Him,
> He is the Great One and Only God.
> The wind of inspiration bends
>   the palm tree of my soul.
> In everything He is a musical chord.

These comprise but a very few examples of the musical metaphors with which the entire collection is pregnant.

I want to point out one other issue regarding *The Grand Harmony*, particularly focusing on the thirty-second poem "Triangulum" and the image of the triangle of faith, hope and love that provide a subtitle. The triangle, of course, is a standard representation of trinity. The image, too, is quite prominent in a series of 11 paintings under the title of "The Triumph of Progress" designed by Polish artist Jan Matejko in the 1880s that are located in the Assembly Hall of Lviv Polytechnic University. There is no question, of course, that during the time Antonych studied and lived in Lviv, he would have seen them. The paintings fuse Christian Biblical allegory with ancient mythology and may have provided a source of inspiration for the poem "Triangulum" in particular and Antonych's collection in general. *The Grand Harmony* quite closely mimics the design and plan of Matejko's paintings. Thus one can posit either an independent mutual source of inspiration through catechetical education of the artist and the poet—or a subconscious or conscious appropriation by Antonych of Matejko's visual representations.

My essential conclusions regarding the collection include the following. Most likely the word "metaphysical" only partly describes one aspect of the nature of Antonych's collection. His poems are really personal intellectual meditations on the imagery and articles of faith of the Bible, the Mass, and church doctrine. The poet is not trying to reach a mystical, intuitive, emotional transcendence in his poems. Rather, his collection is more about rationally defining God, about singing psalms, songs of praise to Him for creating a beautiful and wondrous universe, and also about reconciling himself with gnawing doubts to his own mortality that in moments of human frailty serve to subvert an intuitive understanding of God and the divine harmony of the universe. That may be why he ends the collection with the poem "Salve Regina," which is the title of a Marian hymn sung in the Western church. It also comprises the last prayer uttered in the Latin rosary. The poet needs that mercy, petitioned for in his entreaty to Mary, to keep him continually on the path of faith "in the dust-covered, accursed home" of his heart, as he puts it, in the way he ends the poem and the collection.

The grand harmony for a person of today in the globalized world has become myth. Many in his or her own way seek harmony with him- or herself, with the world, with God. Antonych's meditative collection is one of those paths that can lead others toward achieving that harmony.

– Michael M. Naydan
*Woskob Family Professor
of Ukrainian Studies
The Pennsylvania State
University*

UT IN OMNIBUS GLORIFICETUR DEUS
May the Lord be Glorified in Everything

You've placed a dreadful burden on my shoulders,
and I must carry it without fail.
Dead things are the happiest—of all Saharan deserts
the fire of Your grace burns most intensely.
You've placed the sun on my shoulders.

You've shown my mute eyes a forbidding goal,
a violet sun in the blue treasure chest of the heavens,
but you have failed to give thunder to my lips—just the rustle
of poplars growing solitarily amid quiet fields,
but I categorically need the language of thunder.

I am a miserable, lisping, worthless poet,
how can I utter Your omnipresence
without grand words or praise? You've thrown
the severest of talents onto my back,
in good time because of the silence of lips.

Though I'm walking to the crossroads, to the yellow of the fields,
I will speak with each passer by as though
                                       with a brother: listen, friend,
brush against the stalks of grain and bow
                                       your forehead in thought:
wanderer of dreary days, for the entire universe
is filled with the imprints of His palms, every atom filled.

VENI SANCTE SPIRITUS
Come, Holy Spirit!

Come, come to me, Holy Dove,
begin to play above my desk with bright wings,
fill my heart with the joy of the plenitude of angels
and protect me before the evil of weakness.

I will raise up my downcast head in weariness
from above yellowed folios and papers.
In my heart, as though in a parchment tome,
I will suddenly decipher Your fiery beauty.

Pour out the feeling of boundlessness to the brim,
my earth-bound soul to the very end,
                            covered with dust like the road.
I do not desire the vestibule of paradise, for I know:
how terrifying it is to fall into the arms of God alive.

Grand Reaper of Souls, with your golden scythe
Cut away the weeds and wild grass of doubts from my heart,
so that I stand before the eye of eternity like a steadfast wall,
proud and firm as steel, Your azure knight.

MUSICA NOCTIS
Music of the Night

Light up the torch of the pale moon in the sky,
illuminate the darkness of the night with stars,
let hearts that are sick with loneliness take comfort
when they see thousands of Your worlds.

In a heart wrapped in the scarves of quiet peace,
melodious, harmonious is every tone.
The distance echoes with just barely audible harps,
wind tunes the night with the tuning fork of God.

Like beautiful, ripe summer on spring's rein,
a seasoned fullness has matured in your soul.
Slightly darkened gray colors, just on the horizon
in the distance, is the golden cupola of the setting sun.

The warm summer night high on mountain crests,
wooded peaks rise up in the fragrances of many flowers.
Let us listen to the great concert in the evening as
God places his hands on the piano of the world.

March 23, 1932

DE MORTE I
On Death I

Only later I will bow my head in thought
above the river of life that has passed
and gaze in mute, quiet sorrow
at the river-bed covered with silt.

Only later, perhaps, in forty years or so,
when I am a miserable man, expressionless,
will I shake life's dust
from my torn pilgrim's vestments.

Only later, perhaps, in forty years or so,
as an everyday average person,
will I see truth through the gloom
and cast aside my pilgrim's staff.

An angel will appear and write out
judgment on azure paper with his sword,
death will come and with a silver key
unlock the door of eternity for me.

March 23, 1932

GLORIA IN EXCELSIS
Glory in the Highest

To embrace all people
with great, bright joy,
to shout "hey" to everyone!
To laugh carefree and happily.

To clap in your palm
Like a little child, loudly, robustly.
Today is without purpose,
today everyone is raucous, without fail.

Today all wounds heal,
all the people smile.
Join the choir, sopranos to the front,
Let an angel be the choir's conductor.

Let a song play during the contest,
For this is the greatest of victories.
Today the Lord was born
in the stream of my heart.

March 23, 1932

DE MORTE IV
On Death IV

I am calm as silence on the water.
I have more than enough strength
Not to be fearful even if
a bat looks me straight in the eye.

When its wings begin to quiver above me
and my eyes, filled entirely with blood, sting,
a single solitary word will be
a mute language—death.

For even the black specter of death
Does not put the strings of my soul out of tune.
O Lord, grant that not even an obstinate wave
Will ever be able to bend me.

O Lord, grant that I stand in the contest
like a cliff against the hordes,
That my death be the last
chord of harmony.

March 24, 1932

DE MORTE II
On Death II

I don't know how to ask anyone:
where is she,[8] where is she, where?
Perhaps she is waiting for me just around
the corner on my way home.

I don't know how to say
exactly where she is.
Until like a prankster she finally
drinks me up like a goblet of wine.

Each of us is a brother to life,
No one wants to die
until the night pays the moon a golden ducat,
the deposit of death.

I know the days become worse,
that something wakes us at night.
Let these poems be the cure
for the dread of death.

March 24, 1933

---

8 Death (*smert'*) is grammatically feminine in Ukrainian.

DUAE VIAE
Two Roads

I've searched for you, Lord, on long roads,
I've asked the whipping swift-winged winds: where is He?
I've thought in vain that the wisdom of books
                          will help against the longing,
that it will calm down the thirsting racing
                          of my heart, that it will gratify me.

I've asked all kinds of people I've met about You,
but all of them have failed to show You to me;
I've looked for you in the lowlands, on mountains,
                          on mountain crest spires,
in a peasant's smoky hut, on a lacquered ballroom floor.

In the dark gloom of dusty libraries,
in strange vague letters of an old folio,
in words written once by a learned Greek monk,
but only inert mold of the past has been slumbering in them.

And I have failed to find You, I searched in vain,
                          at least for the possibility,
of seeing Your presence. It is dark all around.
I did not know that the two roads right
                          next to each other had failed to cross:
that you also had been searching for me—
                          in my heart. But also in vain.

March 24, 1932

ARS POETICA II, 1
The Art of Poetry II, 1

I am an ordinary poet,
each day fascinates me.
I do not understand the world,
I do not understand my own songs.

To drink ecstasy to the brim…
A carefree voice like a cricket,
this is the way I sing,
with just the echo still ringing in the mountains.

The beginning of rapture,
of religion and sonnets;
rapture gives birth to our
apostles and poets.

I do not know how to write poems,
I scoff at the rules and standards.
For me it is God Himself
who forms my poetics.

Thursday, March 24, 1932

AMEN

The concert is over,
just the echo is deceptive.
The end of everything is death,
mysterious and unknown.

Both the joyous and sad
pass like a specter.
God is already placing me
like a violin into a case.

The singing is over,
the string's no longer playing.
Let the heart finish singing
what is left unsaid of these words.

You must change your heart
For it to finish singing.
You need very little to reach happiness:
just some harmony.
        Amen.

March 24, 1932

VINEA DIVINA
The Lord's Vineyard

Oh life always has thousands of enticements,
even when it's sad and hard,
though
infinite betrayals hide in each joy.

O, life, so varied in singularity,
O, life, thousand-colored in gray,
though it is just bitter wormwood lying at the bottom
of most happiness.

O, poetry of our everyday affairs,
O, romanticism of our ordinary human laws,
yet a goblet of wine has gathered up
weariness and bitterness.

Oh life has thousands of enticements,
but even when it is sad and hard,
there is just one:
to gather grapes in the vineyard of the Lord.

Friday, March 25, 1932

DEUS MAGNIFICUS
Magnificent God

On the highest crests of mountains—is He,
on the deepest bottom of the sea—is He,
in the sky, in the chambers of mountains—is He,
in every night, in every day—is He.

You hear Him in the rustle of wind and the gurgling sea foam,
everywhere, He is everywhere—Great and Indivisible.
Yet He is greatest inside the most destitute of walls
and in a child's prayer.

When you call in the night—He is there,
when you call for help—He is there,
when you search—He is there,
you already have Him for He is within.

He gives melody to every thing.
He is harmony, He is a musical chord,
He is the tuning fork tuning your heart,
He is Perfect, Majestic Sound.

Friday, March 25, 1932

TE DEUM LAUDAMUS I
We Praise You Lord I

The earth is a million-stringed, golden-stringed harp,
the earth is a million-fleeced, green-fleeced scarf,
the earth is a tiny-toned, silver-pealing violin,
the earth is an unstoppable, all-billowing storm.

Each day is an eternal prayer to You,
each night an eternal psalm to You,
each day is human yearning for the sky,
each night a battle of good and evil.

The sky is a blue roof above the earth,
the sky is an eternal question mark,
the sky is blue like naïveté in eyes,
the sky is the ultimate aim of yearning.

The earth is the golden-stringed harp of Your glory,
day and night—a prayer of longing and hope,
the sky is the ultimate human goal,
all together—the grand harmony glorifies You.

March 25, 1932

ADVOCATUS DIABOLI
Devil's Advocate

When I stand before Your fiery face
peaceful, unyielding,
not fearful for the end of my life,
not quick to repentance,

you'll query me about all my actions,
I'll say something like this:
"My soul has been stained by life and evil,
but look into my heart."

Then you'll place all my pride,
all my love, on the scales,
I'll look without fear, though I wasn't timid,
for my heart will prevail again.

But premature joy is mine,
not very long lasting and illusory,
for suddenly reason will whisper like a snake:
"Your love was malicious."

Friday, March 25, 1933

RESURECTIO
Resurrection

Bells peal in early morning for the morning sun rises
bells peal, they welcome, for the sun is clear.
Bells peal in early morning, from the very dawn,
bells peal, they welcome, spring is rising...

Bells peal without pause, for joy, for glory,
bells peal in a drunken joust, though now grown silent, they
                                      peal again,
bells peal without pause, they awaken dark silence,
bells peal, for love is rising in the heart.

Bells peal inconsolably, they summon the miracle of mystery,
bells peal in silver tones, a stream of joyful words,
bells peal self-pealingly, for this is of the spirit and matter,
bells peal, a harmonic duet is rising.

Bells peal silkily, brilliantly, baroquely,
bells peal, the entire earth rushes to give greeting,
bells peal silkily, they awaken the Sun's Word,
bells peal, for my soul is rising.

Friday, March 25, 1933

MOMENTUM CUM DEO
A Moment with God

How hard, how hard, how hard it is
to find just a single moment
so you can forget everyday life,
so your spirit can fly to the treetops.

For it allures, it entices, it charms,
for life eternally takes prisoners,
a life filled with allure and charm
glitters from false curtains.

Multicolored, frenzied life,
so variegated, different, and new,
it comes to me rapaciously,
it enraptures, deludes, and tears me.

How hard, how hard, how hard it is
for us to forget everyday life,
a single brief moment
to converse with God—one on one.

Friday, March 25, 1933

LITANIA
A Litany

Lord, do You know how much we need faith—
More than our stale daily bread,
do You know our sadness all the way up in heaven,
how the hovel of daily life burdens us?

How we need Your smile,
joy for our hearts,
deliverance from all evil,
how we need sunny faith.

The azure flower of hope,
the great truth-sun at night,
the golden equilibrium of reality and dreams,
the harmony of the soul.

Lord, we need Revelations again,
the autumn rains of doubt lash us.
Let us feel the Tongues of Flame
once again in a burning bush.

Saturday March 26, 1932

A PRAYER

A mortal's prayer is like smoke,
it circles above a village like a white swan,
it blows along the crystal sky
like a curly-haired golden stem.

A mortal's prayer is a Gothic tower
that rises up straight into the azure,
that the rapture of the maestro and pain have embroidered—
the mute prayer is silent above the bustle of the throng.

A mortal's prayer is like a poplar tree,
it looks at the sky above a field of rye,
slim, thin, alone amid the field,
it sways from the wind and quivers.

A mortal's prayer is like an eagle, above the clouds
it flies out from the earth's threshold,
and begins to quiver like a quail:
it catches sight of the fiery face of God.

Saturday, March 26, 1933

WEEKDAY

At five o'clock in the morning
to tear yourself so spiritedly from bed.
It's so joyful, spring-like!
a meadow, a forest, a trail.

It's seven in the morning,
time to go home.
Rye bread for breakfast,
the best cure for weary bones.

The day, the sun at full strength
and the blue platter of the sky.
Waves float slowly;
the usual, gray work.

The dithyrambs of the day grow silent,
The night snuffs out the rose of the sun.
Now I will compose my simple iambs
to give glory to God.

Saturday, March 26, 1932

SACRED SIMPLICITY

The world is great and wide,
a circular horizon all around.
Oh, how it is so wonderful
just to be four years old!

The world plays glimmering,
a boundless, robust world.
Oh, how infinitely happy it is
just to be twenty years old.

Grand simplicity is
the highest perfection.
Naïveté is sacred,
Smallness is the crowning.

This kind of a person is happy.
His road is clear:
like a child
he prays to God in naïveté!

Saturday, March 26, 1932

NAÏVETÉ

Whom does it trouble
that I write poems?
Whether they're good or bad,
It is all the same to Him.

Who is interested
that I write verse?
I would say just one thing to you:
all is for the glory of God.

The door to happiness is small:
rapture and the heavens,
harmony in your heart—
you need nothing more.

Whether the days are good or bad,
The thoughts are peaceful, noble.
I write my naïve poems
for the glory of God.

Saturday, March 26, 1932

ARS POETICA II, 4
The Art of Poetry II, 4

An enrapt full-grown child,
enrapt by beauty,
one of those vagrants
who nourishes himself with the dew.

Enrapt to the brim,
like the color concentrated in a rose.
I have nothing more,
just a cedar harp.

I want to play for Him,
to strum the harp with my hand.
A hundred strings, like silver grating,
with which the cedar is strung.

Time to begin to ring the goblet,
God will embrace me
and will cut the string that was used
with a scythe.

Saturday, March 26, 1932

VENI CREATOR
Come, Creator!

Creator of thousands of moons, millions of stars,
Maestro of the radiant music of the ether,
Your peaceful gaze rises in rays of sun
Into the blackest soul and into the blackest of all caves.

Lord of silence and the roar of storms,
                            the Tuner of day and night,
will we no longer be able to recognize the Sunny Truth?
We raise our troubled eyes to the sky,
But it keeps silent and guards its secrets enviously.

Master of colors and sounds, the fragrance
                            of flowers and the noise of waves,
in every thing You are *Kalokagathia*,[9]
                            You are Goodness and Beauty,
You are the purpose for everything,
                            the greatest, unreachable spire,
O come, Almighty Creator, descend to us like the dew.

You are the chord of cosmic harmony all around us,
I am enharmonic—forced to struggle among the waves:
and when my weak soul should fall downward,
muffle the dissonance and smite a helpless soul with thunder.

Sunday, March 27, 1932

---

9   From the Greek meaning beauty and goodness. It is the ideal striven for by the Greeks, the harmony between body and spirit. I am grateful to Yuri Andrukhovych for enlightening me regarding this.

CONFITEOR
I confess

I have fought with God intently
and did not want to bow my lean brow...
O bountiful squandering of my life!
Haughty pride has led me behind it.

Haughty pride, nimble and bold,
has kept me captive, clasped me in its claws.
I sang of God's creation of the body
and appeal to Him: liberate me from my soul...

Propping myself against my own madness,
I hoped to cross the entire path alone.
Without wavering in the approach of death,
intoxicated with life, you've even pushed away the sky.

But today I am ripe as in summer,
I am done with my youthful pranks and scuffles,
I have made my peace with God and the world,
and have found perfect harmony in my heart.

Sunday, March 27, 1932

MATER DOLOROSA
The Sorrowful Mother

The wind was blowing into the dark,
black night.
Don't count the silver stars;
just three of them are glimmering.

Three lonely stars,
like three tears,
like pearls in the sea,
the wind was blowing.

The black shawl of night
All around like a tent.
But what do your eyes see?
A mother walking along a path.

The hour of darkness,
stars are like yellow grain.
She's walking with her Son's heart
pierced by thorns

Sunday, March 27, 1932

LIBER PEREGRINORUM 3
Book of Pilgrims 3
(Jerusalem)

The yellow road beneath my feet,
the blue sky above us.
I walk along unknown paths.
Man is an eternal pilgrim.

I miss laughter and spring,
the birds are singing above me,
ringing songs soar in a din
before this mute pilgrim.

I carry a burden on my shoulders,
the gift of God in a blue treasure chest,
though the fierce heat of the swelter burns,
though it whips with a vicious lash.

And so I wander without stopping,
I push along every day like rosary beads,
and I will rest only
when I reach Jerusalem.

Sunday March 27, 1932

AVE MARIA
Rejoice, Maria!

I whisper Your resounding name in the morning on a sunny day,
fly to me like song, like an early gentle breeze, like a pearl dream,
fly to me with the first blossoming of the tiny petals of a rose,
tame the quivering of the enharmonic
>   strings of the harp of the heart.

Ave Maria.

My soul is a trodden path on the unknown fields of reality.
the wind of life has already blown dust onto it.
Fly to me, Immaculate Virgin, quietly stand above a poor heart,
With your hand halt the enharmony of this trembling.
Ave Maria.

Your appearance is a dream of paradise, as you walk through
a rustling pine grove, clear, May-like, tender, glittering, like a lily.
Soar and bring a healing cure in a hard battle,
calm the enharmonic gnashing of the heart's harp.
Ave Maria.

Every day in the morning and evening
>   I pensively whisper Your name.

The name is the song of the sun, harmony, hope.
Fly to me, Most-Immaculate Virgin,
>   and drive away evil from me,

place your palm onto a young brow.
Ave Maria.

Sunday, March 27, 1932

GREEN HOLY DAY[10]

Today is the Green Holy Day,
the grass has already turned green.
My soul has been crucified,
today it's alive again.

Everyone rush off to church!
Blow, warm wind, flutter!
I hang green May
on the door of my own soul.

Happiness everywhere, joy, laughter,
like youth it's still eternal.
It seems God Himself is clapping his hands
out of satisfaction.

---

10   The "Green Holidays" occur during the seventh Sunday after Easter in the Eastern Church and coincide with the celebration of the Descent of the Holy Spirit to the apostles on the fiftieth day after the Resurrection of Christ—known as Pentecost in the West. The Spirit appeared to the apostles in the form of fiery tongues to inspire them with the task of spreading the Gospels to the people. In the Ukrainian tradition, churches and the doorways of homes are adorned with branches of leafy trees. Graves of the departed are also adorned with green things to symbolize resurrection. It is also traditional in Ukraine for the house to undergo a major spring cleaning to prepare for the holiday. The holiday's link to nature has its source in ancient pagan rites and a belief in the sacredness of trees and their ability to keep away evil spirits.

Everything moves headlong like a fairytale,
you don't see the world's grime.
I'm also going to clap my hands
along with God.

Monday, March 28, 1932

ON DEATH III
Requiem

Already the hand of an angel has touched your proud brow,
you're sleeping, my friend, in your grave.
For you the contradictions of good and
                            evil already no longer exist,
things evil and things beloved no longer exist.

You have given to eternity what is eternal,
                            and to the earth what is earthly,
and have settled accounts with life.
The Lord's emissary has listed in detail what was bright and dark
in the soul, and you already are happy.

Your white shadow already knows the greatest mystery of all,
it is feasting among eternal conversations.
The heart has gone into the black earth,
                            perhaps, grown into wheat,
and now the universe is your body.

Time has halted—this is God, who has ended your future days.
I'll go right behind you without delay,
And still seek the harmony of life and struggle now—
you already have found the harmony of peace.

Tuesday, March 29, 1932

ARS POETICA II, 2
The Art of Poetry II, 2

To sing of a house
small and poor,
where it's nice for your brother,
where it's joyful to live.

To sing of spring,
wild and wondrous,
heavenly, green,
of a sunny moment.

To sing of sorrow,
as joy overcomes
it, though like a sea;
of the seas of victories.

And also of a moment,
the very highest, the solitary one,
when someone is visited by
God.

Tuesday, March 29, 1932

ARS POETICA II, 3
The Art of Poetry II, 3

For me a day
without songs
is black night
for young eyes.

For me a day
without songs
is like a coffin
that death has fastened.

For me a day
without songs
is like a fog
of pale deceptions.

Look up—
this is just to know:
that for God the day—
is a bouquet made of songs.

Tuesday March 29, 1932

TRIANGULUM
A Triangle
(Faith, Hope, Love)

You desire what is unknown
what is strange
the heart trembles with longing.

The azure flower will fade,
it will drown in the depth,
you lose the desire to live.

Kill sorrow and profound pain
with an arrow,
have faith and hope again.

For happiness is a triangle,
and it has three sides:
faith, hope, and love.

Tuesday, March 29, 1932

THE WOODSMAN, Part 2

O black screech owl, don't hoot
about there just being sorrow everywhere,
for there is a joyful woodsman
chopping his wood with a song.

There is also a cheerful wood splitter,
incessantly battling with life,
he is always cheerful like the oak.
Poet of black hands, sow the seed of joy!

For the day of reward will come, it will come
to the patient, the merciful and the brave.
You no longer will know sad songs.
The greatest happiness is to be good.

To carry joy and love
to poor, to humble, to wretched homes
and to chop so much wood that
no rooms are left unheated.

Tuesday, March 29, 1932

THE FOURTH ANGLE
(Faith, Hope, Love, 2)

Oh, human souls eternally yearn,
time will bring defeat.
Let an angel whisper a new silken fairytale
into our ears.

A silver angel, an unseen specter,
will descend in the night,
above your eyes you'll even see
your shining homeland.

To recognize again the single, most important thing,
to hear the forgotten once again,
and to reach the unreachable,
to attain the unattainable.

Where is the turn to eternity from earth,
tell me, my home!
To find the fourth angle in a triangle is
The Great Unknown.

Tuesday, March 29, 1932

CREDO
I Believe
(Faith, Hope, Love, 3)

Many strings
began to strum
at the bottom of my heart.
I believe in the renewal of the spirit in the spring bath of hope.

Lyres play,
Husk the seed of faith
in the heart.
I believe in the renewal of the spirit through the burning bush.

Many strings
are cut,
o heart, lament.
I believe that a fiery day of new revelation will come.

Many strings
began to strum
all of them began to play.
I believe in the great surprise of the soul.

Tuesday, March 29, 1932

SPES
Hope
(Faith, Hope, Love, 3)

When all around night is black,
life is hard, like a grindstone,
but the heart feels faint from the pain,
you come,
hope.

You bring bright laughter to fate,
illness is slowly cured,
renewal ripens in the heart.
O give us light,
hope.

When our brows are burning up,
our soul is poisoned and weak,
your fresh cold blows,
Soar to us,
hope.

The road meanders, you don't see the sun
from behind the door-step,
despair smolders in the heart,
you come,
hope,
the daughter of God!

Tuesday, March 29, 1932

AGNUS DEI
Lamb of God

You are not a proud gray-winged eagle that blocks the sun in your eyes with its wings like a cloud, You are not a beast of prey, a lion full of strength that evokes terror with its fierce roar all around its den.
>I know Your other name:
>Lamb of God.

You are not wrath, You are not thunder, You are not punishment, but just a hymn, just a house of goodness and the sound of forgiveness. You are not a sword, or fire, or a specter, allow me to read the word of Your hands at the bottom of my heart:
>I call to You every day:
>Lamb of God.

You are not night for us, You are not darkness.
You are the light for eternity, the early morning
>shine in the gloom.

You are not gnashing or dissonance,
You are a bell-pealing chord, the single harmony of the world,
>You are the song of the sun and the bright day:
>Lamb of God.

You are not pain, You are not gnawing moths.
You are love, again you pour joy in our hearts, good Lord.
You are comfort, You are the cure for all evil.
And if the human heart can not endure in poverty,
>It calls a single name in the darkness:
>Lamb of God.

Monday, April 11, 1932

MATER GLORIOSA
Mother of Glory

Play, harps, play, lyres, play lutes, play zitherns,
pour out joy, wash away cares, shroud grief
                          with the mantle of spring.
Let the silver-waved, tiny-grained river beds abundantly splash,
fragrant roses and lustrous pearls of the Lord
                          in golden rain from the heavens.

Play, harps, play, lyres, play zitherns, play lutes,
ring bells, pour sunny and mighty tones,
for the Mother of God is coming out of her
                          blue palace in the sky,
she's dressed in the golden-threaded
                          garments of a seven-colored rainbow.

Play, harps, play, lyres, play, lutes, a silvery song,
rejoice, o rejoice, o rejoice, Mary!
Oh, how can I find the spirited and sweet-sounding words
to express this and sing out what appears in our heart?

Play, harps, play, zitherns, play, lutes, play, lyres.
Oh, with what grand, heaven-reaching, divine tone
will I—alone and gray—be able to express the joy of my heart?
Oh, open up my earth-bound eyes with
                          the chiton of grace and goodness!

May 30-31, 1932

ASCENSIO
The Ascension

The doors of heaven have closed,
as well as the silver gates.
You have emerged into the ether,
Mute sorrow has remained with us.

O, you thorn of despair
that wounds our bare soul!
When, when will the Dove return
hope to us with a twig?

We have read the holy writ,
words are scattered in rubble,
we wait for the ascension
of our impoverished, earthly souls.

The way the sea during a heavy surf
runs from the ring of shores,
every day human yearning for You
soars toward the sky.

APAGE SATANAS
Be gone, satan!

I finger the nights and days like rosary beads, one at a time,
something quietly whispers in my ears,
                         like the rustle of cameo petals.
This is the banished angel on a crystal barrel-organ
playing a sweet song beneath the window of my soul.

"Come, come!" A bright green parrot screams.
"Come, come—here pleasures await, wild and hot."
A nasal owl sarcastically responds from the meadow.
Cold sparks. Eyes already no longer see.

And the whisper floats further, full of sorrow, pain, and fear:
"I, like you, am lonely, unhappy." Ravens caw.
"Take, take in a wanderer and eternal
                         journeyman into your home,
take, take in a poet of rebellion, pleasure and despair.

I will draw a secret sign on your door,
let there be a friendly pact between you and me."
I step out in front of my house and I sprinkle
the threshold of my heart with healing, holy water.

June 1, 1932

TE DEUM LAUDAMUS, II
Let Us Praise the Lord, II

For You the sea plays a radiant, spirited psalm,
for You the wind sings echoing, thunderous songs,
for You the fierce storm disturbs the bottom of the sea,
for You the grass stirs in a silken whisper.

About You the forest tells a quiet, strange, wonderful tale,
about You blue forget-me-nots remember forever,
about You the sun tells of Fiery Newness,
about You an angel whispers a fairytale into a child's ears.

For You the gold of tall, steep cupolas shines,
for You pearl altars burn with incense,
for You poets pay the tribute of inspired words,
for You prophetic zithern players strike silver strings.

About You pagans have waited for revelation through the ages,
about You now the fairytale of distant years still speaks to us,
about You a base lost soul still carries a thought,
about You, good Lord, every human heart dreams.

June 2, 1932

KYRIE ELEISON
Lord Have Mercy!

I lift up my hands in mute ecstasy,
Darkened eyes shine with it.
Give sweet utterance to my lips for You.
> Lord have mercy
> from the silence of night.

With spirited ecstasy earthly eyes burn,
in spirited ecstasy I lift up my hands.
Give the power of the Lord's inspiration to my lips.
> Lord have mercy
> from the mark of despair.

My soul is becoming peaceful and well,
I tear the dark, opaque distance with my eyes.
Give sharp, light-winged language to my lips!
> Lord have mercy
> from the darkness of sight.

I tear the unknown, opaque distance with my eyes,
my soul again is already peaceful and healthy,
Give creative, unbound, apt language to my lips!
> Lord have mercy
> from the feebleness of the word.

June 2, 1932

MAGNIFICAT
Glorification

Sing, my soul, a praiseful psalm to the Lord,
with word-stars, word-pearls, resound and glimmer,
sing, soul, the victory of the bright sun,
with word-roses, word-sparks the holy fire burns.

Sing, my soul, a mighty song to the Lord,
descend to me, Dove-Spirit, and cover me with your wings,
pour your inspired contents into my wretched form,
let the holy fire of ecstasy burn in my eyes.

Sing, my soul, an immaculate song to the Lord,
Oh be joyful, oh rejoice!
Point Your path to ecstatic eyes,
let me become Your harp.

O heart, sing a psalm of praise to Him,
He is the Great One and Only God.
The wind of inspiration bends the palm tree of my soul.
In everything He is a musical chord.

June 3, 1932

ARS POETICA
The Art of Poetry

Hexameters, trochees,
stormy anapests—
this has the luster of a cameo,
it caresses the ear like silk.

Deep assonances,
the refined refrain of sonnets,
and sweet-sounding stanzas—
this is an apothecary of words.

These are fragrant perfumes,
these are wares of glitter.
Poets shape them for women
In the rustle of inspiration.

I know other poems;
though they fail to keep to dictates,
they are no worse than those:
the songs God dictates.

SALVE REGINA
Save us, Queen!

Salve Regina!
The heart awakens and beats,
The human soul awakens from earthly swaddling clothes,
golden-haired stalks of rye fall to their knees,
the horizon removes the sun from the mountains
                             like a hat from your head,
to greet You.

Salve Regina!
Before You
Sunny waves and an angel-herald stream,
before You fragrant roses, violets and fresh hay,
before You our hearts with sorrow
stream.

Salve Regina!
On the blue path of the sky
you ride in a trot in a four-horse carriage,
white as snow, like a child's soul, like sea foam,
a bright-haired coachman—a curly-haired angel—
                             holds the reins in his hand.
Silver-stringed harps play.

Salve Regina!
Where you journey through there is—great change,
Where you journey through—life smiles,
and You will arrive at a meager night lodging,
the dust-covered, accursed
home of my heart.

March 24, 1932

Contents

BIOGRAPHICAL NOTE 7

ANTONYCH WRITING GOD: THE METAPHYSICS
OF THE GRAND HARMONY 11

    UT IN OMNIBUS GLORIFICETUR DEUS 20

    VENI SANCTE SPIRITUS 21

    MUSICA NOCTIS 22

    DE MORTE I 23

    GLORIA IN EXCELSIS 24

    DE MORTE IV 25

    DE MORTE II 26

    DUAE VIAE 27

    ARS POETICA II, 1 28

    AMEN 29

    VINEA DIVINA 30

    DEUS MAGNIFICUS 31

    TE DEUM LAUDAMUS I 32

    ADVOCATUS DIABOLI 33

RESURECTIO	34
MOMENTUM CUM DEO	35
LITANIA	36
A PRAYER	37
WEEKDAY	38
SACRED SIMPLICITY	39
NAÏVETÉ	40
ARS POETICA II, 4	41
VENI CREATOR	42
CONFITEOR	43
MATER DOLOROSA	44
LIBER PEREGRINORUM 3	45
AVE MARIA	46
GREEN HOLY DAY	47
ON DEATH III	49
ARS POETICA II, 2	50
ARS POETICA II, 3	51

TRIANGULUM	52
THE WOODSMAN, PART 2	53
THE FOURTH ANGLE	54
CREDO	55
SPES	56
AGNUS DEI	57
MATER GLORIOSA	58
ASCENSIO	59
APAGE SATANAS	60
TE DEUM LAUDAMUS, II	61
KYRIE ELEISON	62
MAGNIFICAT	63
ARS POETICA	64
SALVE REGINA	65

Pavlo Tychyna:
The Complete Early Poetry Collections

Pavlo Tychyna (1891-1967) is arguably the greatest Ukrainian poet of the twentieth century and has been described as a "tillerman's Orpheus" by Ukrainian poet and literary critic Vasyl Barka. With his innovative poetics, deep spirituality and creative word play, Tychyna deserves a place among the pantheon of his European contemporaries such as T.S. Eliot, Ezra Pound, Rainer Maria Rilke, Federico Garcia Lorca, and Osip Mandelstam. His early collections *Clarinets of the Sun* (1918), *The Plow* (1920), *Instead of Sonnets and Octaves* (1920), The Wind from Ukraine (1924), and his poetic cycle In the Orchestra of the Cosmos (1921) mark the pinnacle of his creativity and poetically document the emotional and spiritual toll of the Revolution of 1917 as well as the Civil War and its aftermath in Ukraine.

Buy it > www.glagoslav.com

Dear Reader,

Thank you for purchasing this book.

We at Glagoslav Publications are glad to welcome you, and hope that you find our books to be a source of knowledge and inspiration.

We want to show the beauty and depth of the Slavic region to everyone looking to expand their horizon and learn something new about different cultures, different people, and we believe that with this book we have managed to do just that.

Now that you've got to know us, we want to get to know you. We value communication with our readers and want to hear from you! We offer several options:

– Join our Book Club on Goodreads, Library Thing and Shelfari, and receive special offers and information about our giveaways;

– Share your opinion about our books on Amazon, Barnes & Noble, Waterstones and other bookstores;

– Join us on Facebook and Twitter for updates on our publications and news about our authors;

– Visit our site www.glagoslav.com to check out our Catalogue and subscribe to our Newsletter.

Glagoslav Publications is getting ready to release a new collection and planning some interesting surprises — stay with us to find out!

Glagoslav Publications
Office 36, 88-90 Hatton Garden
EC1N 8PN London, UK
Tel: + 44 (0) 20 32 86 99 82
Email: contact@glagoslav.com

Glagoslav Publications Catalogue

- *The Time of Women* by Elena Chizhova
- *Andrei Tarkovsky: The Collector of Dreams* by Layla Alexander-Garrett
- *Andrei Tarkovsky - A Life on the Cross* by Lyudmila Boyadzhieva
- *Sin* by Zakhar Prilepin
- *Hardly Ever Otherwise* by Maria Matios
- *Khatyn* by Ales Adamovich
- *The Lost Button* by Irene Rozdobudko
- *Christened with Crosses* by Eduard Kochergin
- *The Vital Needs of the Dead* by Igor Sakhnovsky
- *The Sarabande of Sara's Band* by Larysa Denysenko
- *A Poet and Bin Laden* by Hamid Ismailov
- *Watching The Russians (Dutch Edition)* by Maria Konyukova
- *Kobzar* by Taras Shevchenko
- *The Stone Bridge* by Alexander Terekhov
- *Moryak* by Lee Mandel
- *King Stakh's Wild Hunt* by Uladzimir Karatkevich
- *The Hawks of Peace* by Dmitry Rogozin
- *Harlequin's Costume* by Leonid Yuzefovich
- *Depeche Mode* by Serhii Zhadan
- *The Grand Slam and other stories (Dutch Edition)* by Leonid Andreev
- *METRO 2033 (Dutch Edition)* by Dmitry Glukhovsky
- *METRO 2034 (Dutch Edition)* by Dmitry Glukhovsky
- *A Russian Story* by Eugenia Kononenko
- *Herstories, An Anthology of New Ukrainian Women Prose Writers*
- *The Battle of the Sexes Russian Style* by Nadezhda Ptushkina
- *A Book Without Photographs* by Sergey Shargunov

- *Down Among The Fishes* by Natalka Babina
- *disUNITY* by Anatoly Kudryavitsky
- *Sankya* by Zakhar Prilepin
- *Wolf Messing* by Tatiana Lungin
- *Good Stalin* by Victor Erofeyev
- *Solar Plexus* by Rustam Ibragimbekov
- *Don't Call me a Victim!* by Dina Yafasova
- *Poetin (Dutch Edition)* by Chris Hutchins and Alexander Korobko
- *A History of Belarus* by Lubov Bazan
- *Children's Fashion of the Russian Empire* by Alexander Vasiliev
- *Empire of Corruption - The Russian National Pastime* by Vladimir Soloviev
- *Heroes of the 90s - People and Money. The Modern History of Russian Capitalism*
- *Fifty Highlights from the Russian Literature (Dutch Edition)* by Maarten Tengbergen
- *Bajesvolk (Dutch Edition)* by Mikhail Khodorkovsky
- *Tsarina Alexandra's Diary (Dutch Edition)*
- *Myths about Russia* by Vladimir Medinskiy
- *Boris Yeltsin - The Decade that Shook the World* by Boris Minaev
- *A Man Of Change - A study of the political life of Boris Yeltsin*
- *Sberbank - The Rebirth of Russia's Financial Giant* by Evgeny Karasyuk
- *To Get Ukraine* by Oleksandr Shyshko
- *Asystole* by Oleg Pavlov
- *Gnedich* by Maria Rybakova
- *Marina Tsvetaeva - The Essential Poetry*

- *Multiple Personalities* by Tatyana Shcherbina
- *The Investigator* by Margarita Khemlin
- *The Exile* by Zinaida Tulub
- *Leo Tolstoy – Flight from paradise* by Pavel Basinsky
- *Moscow in the 1930* by Natalia Gromova
- *Laurus (Dutch edition)* by Evgenij Vodolazkin
- *Prisoner* by Anna Nemzer
- *The Crime of Chernobyl - The Nuclear Goulag* by Wladimir Tchertkoff
- *Alpine Ballad* by Vasil Bykau
- *The Complete Correspondence of Hryhory Skovoroda*
- *The Tale of Aypi* by Ak Welsapar
- *Selected Poems* by Lydia Grigorieva
- *The Fantastic Worlds of Yuri Vynnychuk*
- *The Garden of Divine Songs and Collected Poetry of Hryhory Skovoroda*
- *Adventures in the Slavic Kitchen: A Book of Essays with Recipes*
- *Seven Signs of the Lion* by Michael M. Naydan
- *Forefathers' Eve* by Adam Mickiewicz
- *One-Two* by Igor Eliseev
- *Girls, be Good* by Bojan Babić
- *Time of the Octopus* by Anatoly Kucherena
- *Soghomon Tehlirian Memories - The Assassination of Talaat*
-

    More coming soon...

www.ingramcontent.com/pod-product-compliance
Lightning Source LLC
Chambersburg PA
CBHW021131080526
44587CB00012B/1233